MW00466461

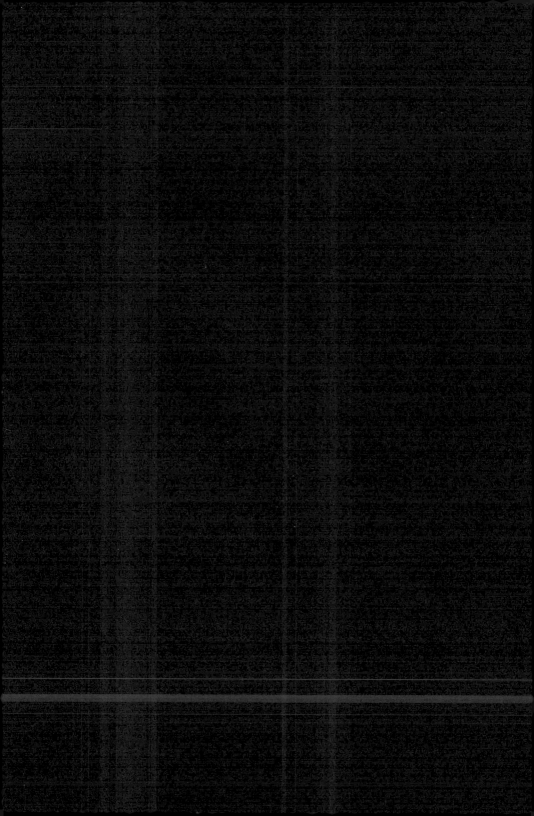

THEORIES OF FALLING

OF

SANDRA BEASLEY

New Issues Poetry & Prose

Editor	William Olsen
Managing Editor	Marianne Swierenga
Copy Editor	Natalie Giarratano
Assistant to the Editor	Kimberly Kolbe

New Issues Poetry & Prose
The College of Arts and Sciences
Western Michigan University
Kalamazoo, MI 49008

First Edition, 2008.

ISBN-10   1-930974-74-4 (paperbound)
ISBN-13   978-1-930974-74-6 (paperbound)

Library of Congress Cataloging-in-Publication Data:
Beasley, Sandra
Theories of Falling/Sandra Beasley
Library of Congress Control Number: 2007939673

Art Director	Tricia Hennessy
Designer	Brent Casanova
Production Manager	Paul Sizer
	The Design Center, Frostic School of Art
	College of Fine Arts
	Western Michigan University
Printing	Cushing-Malloy, Inc.

THEORIES OF
FALLING

SANDRA BEASLEY

New Issues

WESTERN MICHIGAN UNIVERSITY

For my family, for giving me this space.
For vagabond loves—you know who you are—
and the love that stayed.

Contents

Acknowledgements:

My thanks to the journals in which earlier versions of many of these poems appeared:

32 Poems: "Cherry Tomatoes" and "American Thing"
Blackbird: "You" and "Drink"
Barrow Street: "Theories of Falling" and "August"
Blue Fifth Review: "Holiday" and "In Which No One Gets Hurt"
Coconut: "Fireproof," "The Angels," and "My Los Alamos"
Delaware Poetry Review: "The Parade"
Dogwood: "The General"
Drunken Boat: "Heretic"
Eleventh Muse: "Unflown"
Foursquare: "Theories of Non-Violence"
Inkwell: "Allergy Girl VI" and "The Puritans"
melancholia's tremulous dreadlocks: "The Story of My Family"
National Literary Review: "Metro Section, Page 4"
New Orleans Review: "This Silver Body"
No Tell Motel: "Allergy Girl I," "Allergy Girl II," "Allergy Girl VII," and
    "Allergy Girl VIII"
Passages North: "Allergy Girl III," "Allergy Girl IV," and "Allergy Girl IX"
Pebble Lake Review: "The Field" and "The Flood"
Poet Lore: "The Door"
The Potomac Review: "Of Mothers"
RHINO: "The Fish"
RUNES: "The Experiment"
The Mangosteen: "Allergy Girl V" and "The Story of My Family"
    (reprinted)
Texas Poetry Journal: "Of Daughters"

"Cherry Tomatoes" was included in the *2008 Anthology of Younger Poets*, published by Outside Voices.

"The Green Flash" was part of a group of poems that received the 2006 Elinor Benedict Poetry Prize, selected by John Poch, from *Passages North* at Northern Michigan University.

"Unflown" received the third place 2006 Lois Beebe Hayna Award from *Eleventh Muse* and was nominated for a Pushcart Prize.

"Small Kingdom" was first published as Tinyside #30 in the *Tinyside* series by Big Game Books in Washington, D.C.

"The Angels" was included in *Online Writing: The Best of the First Ten Years*, published by Snowvigate Press.

These poems would not exist without the guidance of my teachers at the University of Virginia and American University. My appreciation to Vermont Studio Center, Virginia Center for the Creative Arts, the Indiana University Writers' Conference, the Jenny McKean Moore Workshop, and the Millay Colony for their support and time in which to write. And to LR, KD, NI, MJ, MM, ST, FL, DA, ME, CS, EM: Thank you, thank you, thank you.

The Experiment

Cherry Tomatoes

Little bastards of vine.
Little demons by the pint.
Red eggs that never hatch,
just collapse and rot. When

my mom told me to gather
their grubby bodies
into my skirt, I'd cry. *You
and your father*, she'd chide—

the way, each time I kicked
and wailed against sailing,
my dad shook his head, said
You and your mother.

Now, a city girl, I ease one
loose from its siblings,
from its clear plastic coffin,
place it on my tongue.

Just to try. The smooth
surface resists, resists,
and erupts in my mouth:
seeds, juice, acid, blood

of a perfect household.
The way, when I finally
went sailing, my stomach
was rocked from inside

out. Little boat, big sea.
Handful of skinned sunsets.

9

Of Daughters

For Christina

When you asked about Persephone, I offered dutiful myth:
shadow queen, six seeds, a season underground.

How could I know it was Demeter's rage you craved,
that shake of grain and sky beneath a mother's fist?

How could I have missed when you first folded your arms
across your chest, not to keep us out but to gather us in?

I should have warned how truth, in this house, is a parasite.
A fever with teeth. Instead I counted out the horses, four,

and the fiery chariot they drew. The art of being rescued.
How your sorrows burrowed in above the bone and bloomed,

juice matriculating into white, rounded flesh. And we called it
coming-of-age. How we bought satin to hold them up, cotton

to dress them down. How we swept deodorant under your arms
to stop the skin from weeping. How we called it victory.

Holiday

The tree is a spruce monster, refusing to fit—
so my father decapitates it with a handsaw.
We drape the body with tinsel before
he weaves in bulbs, their white and steady light,
and sneaks in his blinkers of blue and green.
This year there are strikes: my sister refuses
to open her advent calendar until he sees a doctor;
my father refuses to see a doctor, popping Excedrin;
my mother votes for a cruise, her sister's house,
anywhere she won't have to hang ornaments.
We thumb through her maps and clippings
but it's that familiar silver that fills our palms,
tinsel we'll be picking from the carpet until May.
On the Eve we open one gift, make one toast, feast:
curried vegetables, green beans and bacon,
wine and more wine, always a knife sharp enough
to cut the roast of our hearts. A lover said *I've never*
seen people trying so hard to make each other happy
manage to make each other so miserable. Clearly, I said,
you do not understand the true meaning of Christmas.
Tonight we'll wrap gifts until dawn, alone
in our many rooms. The house quiet except for
my father's cough; except for twenty-five chocolates
rattling behind twenty-five unopened windows;
except for my sister stringing up angels, in one hand
their tiny napes of neck and in the other hand, a hook.

The Green Flash

My father says that when the yellow sun meets the blue sea
at clearest dusk, you can see a green flash.
Even now I turn my eyes dutifully to the horizon.

I always flipped to the last page first.
I swallowed watermelon seeds, then waited. I split open a family
of Matroyshka dolls and tapped the baby's head,
hoping it too was hollow.

If you sealed a cat in a box and never peeked it would live forever,
but I'd be picking at the lock by day two.
I read about Orpheus and stood in front of the mirror,

glancing over my shoulder just to see Eurydice drop away.
I studied Houdini's act: easing chains, slipping knots,
never revealing the secret of his escape. How could he

resist? I liked a trick, but what I loved was the reveal.
In his office, my mother found the roll of photographs—
twenty-one images of smiling fidelity—and stopped there.

Not me. I wanted to see those other three frames.
I dug around for the negatives. I went to the window.
I held my father up to that ruthless sun and looked, and looked.

The Experiment

My mother mixed sugar and water in a jar.

I laid the thin sheet of cotton down on garden stone.

Her brush trailed islands across the paper—

one, two, a Fiji, a Hokkaido,

coastlines she'd seen only in magazines—

while I caught eight caterpillars and hunkered down,

cupping their fuzzy, blind blue, and as she lifted her brush

I fed them onto the edge of the page.

Then, a bath. A card game. Sandwiches. Braiding.

Years later, she'll say she had never wanted children.

When we checked again the caterpillars were gone,

sugared spots chewed away. *Our map of hunger,*

she said, holding the latticed sheet up to the sun—

light casting an archipelago across her face.

Of Mothers

One cleaned house by throwing things from
the attic window: a sock, a bear, a record, a toaster.
One was wiretapped by the FBI

One took another man into her husband's bedroom,
then closed the door. One got drunk
before marinating all the meat in the fridge.

One sits at the craft fair, selling silhouettes:
black vellum that yields to her scissors to create
a church, a barn, a field of daisies, an intricate paisley.

Her daughter sits quiet, slicing paper dolls from tissue.
She's maybe six. She bites her lower lip as she carves
the fat, triangular skirts, clipping wedges

for hands that will hold. When she reaches out for
another cookie her mother slaps her wrist.
The girl's eyes well with tears. Say you love me,

then cut a thousand times. But promise
you'll unfold me with slow hands. Promise me
what remains will be a shape of beauty.

The Story of My Family

You're a tooth I tongue and tongue,
tasting blood as you loosen,

testing the sweet root of the hole.
The shudder and catch, the god spit,

and though I dip the bone in gold,
no lover wants to wear a necklace

of you. Carry you in my pocket
and you smolder. Sow the field with you

and you sprout in hours, white tips
thrusting through the meal soil—

one book says a bean pushes its husk
away, hauling the used body to the surface;

one book says the army is born whole,
fingers scratching toward any light.

Allergy Girl

Wasting. A hunger so great I bite through a pacifier.
My mother tries to fix me with *more milk, more milk*.
Doctors run tests on my squalling body. No breast
is safe, no cowgoatsoy milk. I nurse on apple juice.

My parents agree on one rule: *Don't break the baby*.
They pour quarters into the arcade game of adulthood,
working the mechanical claw right, left, right, back,
aiming for the stuffed bear, missing. A clutch

of cheesecake. A buttermilk biscuit. Each time
my lips swelling, breath skipping. They pace the E.R.
Did we break the baby? My mother dissects labels:
casein, protein, lactylate. Easier to cook from scratch.

My father perfects *Shhh, it's not that bad, you can breathe.
Breathe.* They cradle me in Benadryl. That's the secret
of marriage: bleary silence in white rooms. Too busy
not-breaking me to take the wrecking ball to each other.

***

Each food was a shape eyed by the antibody,
looking for an immunoglobulin hole to match.
A good fit would make for a bad reaction.

My bloodstream was a Fisher-Price workbench,
full of exact and waiting geometries.
I was a lot of good fits waiting to happen.

Peanuts tumbled by, harmless. But a cashew—
that fit into the open crescent, *there*, its immune
goblin hole. My antibodies had their plastic red

histamine hammers ready—*smack smack
smack*—skin of my forearms, chin, chest
rippling out with each little blow—

They were just doing their job.

***

In the community kitchen she offers her cup and when I say no,
when I admit I've never trusted soup—all that cream,

mushroom, miso, reconstituted noodles—when I mention that Boston girl,
dropped dead in a spill of peanut broth from a sidewalk ladle—

Maggie shakes her spoon at me. She says *Jesus, when's the last time*
you just shut your eyes and went along for the ride?

August. Age eight. I know this because in September, age eight,
first day of school, I will report that for my summer vacation

I rode the Magic Mountain rollercoaster and fell out. I will swear
the lapbelt came clear off on that final hill, the one

lit by a neon green moon. I will explain how I hung on,
how it took a half hour to save me. How I shook the big white hand

of Mickey himself. How we now had season passes.
What I recall is not the lie, or how many times I told the lie,

or how many kids called me out on the lie. What I recall
are those long minutes: dangling, steel tracks digging into my fingers.

August. Same summer I took to filling bowls from the hot tap, sipping
water black with pepper. September, when I started carrying

my own Benadryl. Age eight. How quiet the hollow mountain.
How happy I was, swallowed in that rich and greasy dark.

***

Praise to the boy who threw dandelions
to prove he loved me. Praise sneezing.
Praise eating the insides out, burrowing
past an egg-brushed crust to pinch bits
of Italian bread. Praise peeling away
fried skin for three bites of chicken. Praise
to the teacher who called me *Little Mouse*.
Praise to the janitor who, each year, mowed
on the same day we ran the mile in P.E.
Praise cut grass, wheezing, a doctor's note.
Praise being in charge of the stopwatch.
Praise to Karen, crossing the finish line
and tackling me with a hug, rubbing
her forearms against mine, licking my cheek.
Praise to Karen, who said *I hate the mile,*
and whatever you are, I hope you're catching.

***

Stacking bowls. Cupping flour.
Greasing the square pan with
sunflower margarine. At twelve,
I am safe if I stick to the surfaces
of baking. When my mother's back

is turned I trespass, caressing
the mixer, settling a knife in the butter.
I tap an egg to the bowl's hungry lip,
stop at the half-crack. She is the one
who makes the cake's heart beat—

pouring milk, whipping in vanilla,
taking yolks from whites. I'm charged
with the toothpicks, foil, arranging
pink sugar letters, pebbled with yellow,
that spell out *Happy Birthday*.

I balance the pan in both hands
all the way to school, picturing
my whole class with plates out,
singing the high tones of duty. Before
our teacher divvies it up, careful

not to touch me. Before someone says
I ought to try a slice, *at least the frosting*,
and gets shushed. Before they watch
as I line up twelve birthday gumdrops
in the pencil groove of my desk.

***

You need to go on the Nebulizer. No.
No. I was ten. *If you don't, we'll use
the EpiPen.* A needle that could shoot
through denim. So I gave in
to that high altitude taste, oxygen
constellated with epinephrine.
A sound rushing, insistent.
They fitted green straps over my ears.
All I could think of were those masks
that drop from the airplane's ceiling
when you fall more than five hundred feet
in one second. *That's it.* My mother
a stewardess, perfect and distant. *Relax.*
They fed me sky until my lips grew cold.

Now, I have learned to be a bad patient.

I refuse IVs. I knock back two Benadryl
with vodka, asleep before asking
anyone to check, each hour, for breath.
When that long itch starts up my throat
I buy a large fries, scarf them down,
sure this greasy mash will shield
my stomach from the egg or melon
or milk protein. Same as that
doomed girl in 14C who knows
her plane is plummeting, is impatient
for the crash, but still sneaks the shade
shut between her and the ground rushing
toward glass double-paned for her safety.

***

While the director fusses over the setting light,
while the stuntman flares a motorcycle's engine,
Harvey Blaine says *Here*, teaches me to ease down
wide, along the tailbone, quick to settle

my shoulders on the bed of nails. This is nothing
like the TV version, Fuji flesh speared by gravity.

No worse than the scratch tests at six, at fifteen:
that slow matrix of pinpricks across my back,
then the essences applied: egg, soy, cat,
dust, roses, five by five to the small of my spine.

The key, the magician says, *is distribution of pressure*.
An egg will hold up to the full squeeze of your fist,
unless you wear a wedding band—uneven moment,
metal push—shell giving way to a bleed of yolk.

One needled point is all it ever took: lactose
blooming to a cluster of welts clear down my thighs.

My shirt is all wrong for this, a thin swath of black
lined only in the front, cleavage-cut for the camera.
Harvey tells me to rise before I feel the blood rise.
The director says *Smile. Look like you enjoy it.*

***

I try not to tell them at first
or if I do, to cut them off.
Even breast milk? Even pot smoke?
Yes. Even you. Yes, you.

The one who had a mouthful
of chocolate without telling me,
taunting *I guess not so sensitive*
before I turned on the light
to a collarbone covered in hives.

The one who could cook
omelets, macaroni, lamb in mango reduction,
who called my friend from his kitchen.
You're gonna have to help me here.

The one who lit his American Spirits,
asked for my roster of old lovers
and, when I teared up
not from the litany but from tobacco,
Oh God, I'm an ass, kissed me upon each
watery red eye.

It's a defense mechanism.
It's a non sequitur.
It's a psychosomatic nightmare.
It's a vaudeville act.

The one who walked me to the library
after our first dinner date. Café Europa
used goat milk in the pita. He'd touched me
with feta on his fingers. I smiled tightly.
He rounded the corner. I called the ambulance.

The same ex who admitted,
when I visited him last week,
I've been eating cottage cheese and yogurt
to ensure a G-rated goodbye.

***

Buttered sandwich, coffee
and cream, cake laced

with chocolate. Each night
this same story, in which he says

I love you, in which he says
I'm tainted. I don't wait

for him to wash up. He scatters
his touch down my body

like Hansel with his crumbs,
sure he will find a way home.

I try to ignore the red hives
rising where his lips have been,

where his fingers have been,
not like dry bread at all, but

like the red-capped mushrooms
that must have later sprung up

in each spot of marked dirt,
newly rich with rotted yeast.

25

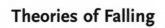

Theories of Falling

You

You are the whole building on fire.

You are the voice of sirens. You are

the dumb crowd milling, the capture

of Weegee's lens. You are flames

licking up the escape. You're the hovering

of a mother at the cliff of her window ledge.

You are the choice to drop her baby.

You're the chance of a beckoning crowd,

six hands gripping a sooty raincoat. You

are the only option. You're a simple drop.

Ten stories below they pray you're like a cloud,

soft floating. You are like a cloud. Grey

and you don't hold anything. You are

that moment before a falling, the falling,

a whir of falling, a wail of falling, the sweet

thud. You are black blood flaring

across the concrete. You are a needle

to the groove of a very sad song.

The whole building burns with you.

American Thing

This light is heavy. This light is a slab
of bacon falling to the meathouse floor.

You believe the methadone will help you.
I believe a three course meal can be

microwaved. This room holds my bed and
my kitchen. This is our nineteenth date.

The right side of your face has been numb
for three weeks. Your fingers prod

at the slack cheek, muscle on bone
as thing on thing. You are trying

to love the body that leaves you. I
watch in the quiet bed. I get up

to reheat the Tinkling Bells Pork.
When I come back, your hand waits

open in the crease of my pillow.
I ease my head upon your palm and lie

to face you, balancing the plate
on the oyster-clasp of our hips. Grease

sizzles and cools. When we finally sit up
you will squeeze the crook of your arm,

as if the pus were some exotic sauce.
Outside, a fast storm will fall—snow

holding clean, untouched. Before the city notices. Before anyone goes anywhere.

The Birches

These woods teem with runaway brides,
birches shedding their white veils.

It must be a dream—you are here,
taller than me, walking far ahead,

arms swinging with momentum.
Ferns curl into fists at my touch.

Moss weeps glycerin. You lean your palm
to a bulging trunk and even from here,

I feel the throb of fungus under bark.
Black flies buzz my ear. In a downed oak

a sack of bagworms pulses, gestating,
blind to how their home has fallen.

I walk faster. I run. This isn't my dream.
Now these woods rise with the dead,

birches tearing off their white shrouds—
hunting down those dumb lovers

who didn't check their breath before burial,
who mourned, who moved on.

The birches shake dirt from the dark roots
of their curls. They sob from spongy trunks,

How dare you leave me? You're nowhere
to be seen, Tom. They speak for you.

Fireproof

Leaving you was a matter of walking away, I thought,

then walking further. His grease, teeth, his wolf breath: I took him in.

What if there was wine? There was wine. What if there was vodka?

It wasn't that much wine. What if he had a gun?

There was no gun. I took him in and trotted back to you, obedient,

holding this sin like a dead bird in my mouth, dropping it at your feet,

this gift. Now make the bitch of me, my love:

Turn loose my eyes, let my jaw drop. My tongue, a leash on the bad mutt.

These marble knuckles, fatty and loud. Punch the sweat

from my collarbone—rainwater off a cheap awning, blood untunneling.

Evict me. I am stubborn with tenants no one will miss.

I am a basement of dumb boiler parts, sometimes mistaken for a plan.

I am down to my last lightbulb, landlord pounding at the door

with your fists, your voice: Even fireproof buildings have their escapes.

Even the tame dogs dream of biting clear to the bone.

In Which No One Gets Hurt

A tasseled girl holds an ace over her heart. My sister covers her eyes.

A spit of lead splits the card. Cameras zoom in on her smile—*Ta-da*.

For TV, my sister says, they rim the barrel with powder for a big spark.

Give over the gun. Give over the girl. The boy gives over the gun.

My sister tapes bags of ketchup under her arm. She loads the blank.

She waves her hand so fast through flame that it does not singe her.

As the magician lowers his circular saw, she flops her legs for show.

My sister says she knows what she's doing. The boy waits in the car.

Officer, the lucky rabbit's foot must have stopped this bullet.

In green light of 3 AM my sister asks *You are single, right?* Look:

Nothing up his sleeve. But a dove that will suffocate if he holds her.

In Which I Fail, Again, to be Vestal

Her body is a temple—

by which I mean monks
sluice her floors clean
with buckets of wastewater;

by which I mean her toenails
glitter, her skin freckled in marble,
sparrows nesting behind her ears;

by which I mean the crease
between breast and rib is anointed
with sweat and safflower oil

in which she bathes her
confessional twice a week,
untangling her sacraments;

by which I mean I envy her.
This body could be a temple
but would rather have its ass

slapped: the only gild on my calf
a rising bruise of bite marks.
I am the dog at her front gate

whining after the gutter fight,
lapping what washes down
those stone steps with a tongue

afraid to know its name.

The Field

I read the note. I crush the fly. I spin the chair. I sit up,
I sit down. I drink the wine. I am crowded with you,

you who sleeps on the floor, puts ketchup on strange things,
who once slapped our hands so hard to the wall I can feel

a knot here, still. There is an art to lingering.
There is nothing in this room except for one girl

and a smudge of black wings. I lie down, I get up.
I put on my best skirt, and no shoes. I drink the wine.

I let the horses out, then wish I had ridden them first.
I walk to the field. Goldenrod flirts along the edges,

monarchs lay their burning wings down: these things
would not impress you. The mower has been by,

his grin of blades, and chopped thistle punches every step.
A hundred yards to the rise where I can see three valleys;

it's the left one that summons the curve of your back,
the thick of it, rough skin you had me trace with my finger.

Every body has a stretch we cannot see or reach on our own.
This is a design flaw and yet, our need for each other.

Thirty yards more to the spot. The thorns have noticed—
now there is earnest biting, now there will be scratch marks,

now my feet will end up weeping again. I can't help it, you
know me—this is the only way I ever cross a field.

The Fish

Bullet dodged, meant your thrust. Another: *Load the gun.*

You bit my shoulder and I thought *Turn, turn and fire—*

those nights we barely surfaced from sleep to go at it,

pulling each into the other's half-dreamed agenda: *Liftoff.*

Touchdown in ten yards. Umbrella, unfurling in hard rain.

For two months I felt the drift of your hand to my thigh

as *fish, fish, fish*, Japanese tails muscling through unseen water.

Always, the body just an alias for something more urgent—

one morning sex was a fist pounding on the submarine hatch;

once you reported our fuck rescued a dozen Croatian children.

Once you tried to call it *making love* and I said *I don't think*

that counts, what we do. Now my room is silent, save for

three fish plucking their gold mouths at the water's skin.

They make it look easy—that blind gasp for something

you need. O, O, O. They make it look like breathing.

Unflown

The men I've loved best have all been mute and brambled, long flat lands

good for hiding and being hidden, good in their fierce silences,
calloused hands laid on the back I turned to them. Burial

is easy alchemy—always this shroud of words. Faith
in the turning, dirt in the end.

You do not want me to turn the spade in you. You do not want
your roots disturbed. You do not want me telling you

what you want. Once, a lover told me he was ready to leave by packing
my suitcase, tying the laces on my running shoes, right and left,

to keep them matched tight. He pressed a ticket's crimped blue edge
into my cut palm. *Here, let me do that,* you say,

and how fresh and cool the glossed paper feels even now

as you unslide the wound, untie the knot, turn the dirty blade
under the spigot. You want the whole day here, unflown, my breast

hulled by your hand, my hips to your hips. You want the baptism of sleep,
the hardest science. You want to know what I want. I want to know

how we turn out like this—
unable to tell a sown field from an untarred runway.   39

Theories of Falling

After years of research, I can only guarantee

that if you go over Niagara in a kayak, you will die.
A ball of chicken wire and quilts? You might make it.
Oak barrel? You'll walk away,
though just to die in a poor house ten years later.

The odds drop above the eighth floor window yet
even from 30,000 feet, a canopy of trees may catch you.
Luck comes to fighter pilots and Czech stewardesses.

Rotoscope cameras have captured the cat as he swivels
first head, then spine, aligns his hind legs, arches
for impact. He turns this helix over and over
until the ground rises to meet him. He bounces.

We do not bounce.

Not that we don't have a knack for certain kinds of falling:
bringing a man home after five rounds of bourbon
because the snow piled up, and he has no coat.
Leaving three friends to try hailing a taxi to Virginia
while he burrows for warmth and says

You're so good, you're so good to me—
hands diagramming every curve, a kind
of sleepy, lustful mathematics. Swivel your head,

align your legs. See if you can land on your feet.

Sometimes an elevator cable does snap—
there is an immediate heat,
the squeal of atoms torn away.
As you hurtle toward bottom you may think
If I time this right, I can be in the air when it hits.

From the outside we see this makes no difference—
what matters is speed relative to the earth, not
the floor of the elevator. But you are not outside.
You're in the cage, bracing your knees,
blood coiling in your heels. So go ahead—

Jump, for God's sake.
Jump like your life depends on it.

The Parade

I throw a parade of thirty reasons you shouldn't love me.
Shut up, you say, *I know what I love*.
What can you know? I know

only that there is no constancy to this body—
I am gaseous, vapor, water and solid. I swell. I shrink.
I bloat. My heels are hardening as we speak.

I run off an ounce of sweat, then gorge on bread and oil.
I claim my nails are short yet manage to claw you.
I call my hair long, but geometry dictates that strands must be

growing every possible length in between.
Shut up, you say. *Come to bed*.
Do you know that when I lay down, the loosening muscles

cause me to grow an inch taller?
Love, please listen to me, I am trying to help you.
Love, you are wasting these elephants and this ticker tape.

Small Kingdom

Who doesn't love a small kingdom?
The lion has her pride, the mole
her starnosed tunnel. My mother
grows three kinds of basil, and I
collect movie stubs in a box marked
Memories. A whelk knows only

the golden ratio of its chambers,
its figure 8 of nerve endings—
drawbridge mantle, moat ocean.
Washed up, its perfect enclosure
reeks of salt. I sort by color.
I file by coast. I know a man

by the cans and coffee cups
he leaves in his car, the thick
puppy mess of him. Who doesn't
dream of cleaning out her small
kingdom, tilting the whole stable
on its Augean edge? Who doesn't love

the disaster of her own making?
Boy, give up your slow reach
before I try to fix your life, before
I let your shell jangle to dust
in my pocket, before I burn
your operculum gate for incense.

I don't know how to keep you
without killing you a little—the way
my mother pares down the rosemary
each year to keep its flavor bright.
The way we must make all loves smaller
before they can enter our kingdom.

43

This Silver Body

The Puritans

Every New England child alive &
enrolled in May 1993 has the same
solar eclipse scorched into her retina:

They line us up on the blacktop,
under the basketball hoop, hand out
pinhole viewers cut from cereal boxes

& say *don't look. Don't look.*
Now. Look now.   Now   stop.
And of course my whole science class

keeps staring, we who have watched
anoles lose one tail and grow another,
who have learned to diagram & spell

endoplasmic reticulum. I squint
through cardboard emblazoned
with the Froot Loops toucan.

No ring of fire so much as a fist,
hovering in front of a bare light bulb.
That must be the hand of God, I think.

I can't place His forearm. *Class,*
inside now. Could the punch
be coming straight at us?

The Angels

They have two noses; six eyes in the arch of each foot.
They never tire of blinking down at the Americans—

our surfboards, machine guns, our dancing hamsters.
The way we shower every day, then rub more oil into our skin.

One notes *There is no end to the number of things*
they can hydrogenate. One checks the spaces in bubble wrap

to see if we store useful things inside. Every April
two men create a thing; then the fruit flies start dying.

By each November one man has a button, and four thousand men
have the job of making sure he does not push the button.

One angel notes *There is no end to the number of buttons*.

One visits a hundred random bedrooms. His third ear
records that *Oh, God* is still popular. He notes a rise

in couples sleeping side by side, holding hands tightly.
He calls this the *Red Rover, Red Rover* position.

Four are assigned to the homeless and ten to schoolteachers,
who tend to jump from bridges more often. The one

in charge of soldiers sketches the long beard of Mr. Maupin,
who swore he wouldn't shave until his son came home.

Mr. Maupin sleeps in a blue recliner, still in his fishing vest:
one pocket stuffed with lures, the other with laminated

baseball cards of his son Matt's face. The backsides
show an angel, all cookie-cutter wings and halo,

yellow ribbons for hair, declaring *Not one left behind*.
The angel sighs and goes to sip whiskey with the angel

of telemarketers. Every night they watch lights dance
across thousands of blue screens *as if*, they note, *constellations*.

Every night they listen to the click of our million keyboards,
toasting the sound American souls make as they collide.

Metro Section, Page 4

For Big Ryan, November 18, 2005

I didn't know you'd left grad school,
joined up, didn't know your first name

was really Donald. *Came under
heavy fire in Ubaydi*. I read *fire*

& think absurdly of a red blanket,
as if the insurgents tucked you in,

& though I know you have died,
how you must be hating the desert.

When your dorm room had no a/c,
you declared Rogers 100 was *Hotter*

than two rats fucking in a wool sock.
How many years? Five? Seven?

I was nothing to you, the girlfriend
of a friend. Already the you I picture

smudges, stenciled over by the Marine
you became: hair clipped at the temples,

a ROTC T-shirt you probably never wore.
You are quoted, months ago, as saying

*Dad, if I die, I did it doing my duty
and protecting my country.* History

is a hand folding over you,
a magician stealing the coin.

Theories of Non-Violence

A frightened rabbit kicks its hind legs so hard that it can

break its own back. Someone thought to record that pain

on tape. Someone said *Shelve this under non-violent tactics*.

Just a line item, buried in daily reports from the siege:

after blasting Ozzy Osbourne and dentist drills, before using

flash bombs and gunfire, they played *Rabbit death scream*.

Repeat loop. Officers wrote the wail was like a teakettle's whistle,

but endless. My father, in uniform, used to speak of war

in terms of the sword and the scalpel. *Scalpel*, meaning we kill

only who we meant to kill. Meaning, *clean*. Meaning, *better*.

Sword, meaning we kill anyone who gets in the way.

Even now, watching news of each new explosion, I wait

to see if our flag flashes onto the screen. If not there's that tiny,

cool blink. *Well then*. An old lover calls to tell me they finally

made him a doctor. *First do no harm*, they made him swear.

Then they said *To save that man, you'll need a sharper knife*.

The General

He fondled a piece of paper
planning for twenty-three thousand deaths,
nodded, *okay*, signed his name.
Later he packed every set of socks
and underwear he owned, knowing
most war criminals are captured
in Laundromats. Instead
a Japanese exchange student
spotted him in a Toronto diner, eating

bacon with eggs sunny side down.
Once they arrested him, wrists in chains
were not enough: they wanted his shoes,
his tropical fish, manicure scissors kept
by his rented bed, the bag of plums
he had planned to eat that night.
They wanted everything he had ever
wanted locked away. When he whined
in his cell, asking if anyone could spare

an aspirin or had news of his daughter,
they hated him for this weakness.
It was a trick, they knew.
According to reports he always spat,
paced, his favorite phrase *sonofawhore*.
He was contagious, bone-cancerous
and cruel; black sludge that masqueraded
as spine marrow, could keep a body walking
for two months, three, before collapsing

under its own shadow. He was much better
as metaphor than man, they decided. Much more
useful. The key made a satisfying *plunk*
as they threw it away. Newspapers loved
the part about plums and Oscar,

the beta my father carefully raised
on cubed worms and AmQuel drops,
trailing a red fin as he made the rounds
of his small glass world.

My Los Alamos

My soybeans for your silo,
My pitcher for your infielder,
My roller skates for your cherry bomb,
My first date for your Dairy Queen.

My chute for your ladder,
My coyote for your anvil,
My Chevy for your Mustang,
My Nancy for your Sherlock.

My cops for your robbers,
My secret for your coat lining,
My equation for your explosion,
My grandfather for your enemy.

My motherhood for your mother.
My childhood for your child,
My boy for your girl,
My girl for your girl.

My tongue for your knee,
My breasts for your tonsils,
My belly for your big toe,
My feet for your elbows.

My underground for your flight.
My uniform for your atom bomb,
My piece for your war,
My peace for your war.

My dance for your Siberia,
My flowers for your tundra,
My flour for your silo,
My hand for your forgiveness,

My hand for your forgiveness,
My hand for your forgetting,
My first date for your Dairy Queen,
My thinking a fist could forget.

The Flood

Soon they will take the blue mask off your face.
Soon they will unzip your thickening blood.
The only bible on hand is *Reader's Digest*
and I study "The Latest Medicine," "Drama in Real Life":

A man walks forty miles after being mauled by a bear.
I am Joe's Lungs. Caught
in her fractured car, a woman lasts a week on two potatoes.
I am Jane's Esophagus.

Soon they'll take to pricking your toe with a ballpoint pen.
Then they'll hand me that pen and ask *Sign here, please.*
And here. Over and over
I read about Johnstown in 1889—ten inches of rain

dropped in one day. As a dam bulges,
there's always someone on duty to look to the valley.
He sees what will follow: the stone bridge that'll collapse
and pulverize rail cars, the ironworks fated

to crown people in barbed wire as they burn.
Soon they will tell me *We only receive what we can bear.*
There's always someone whose job is to ring the alarm,
but be honest: there's no plan for sixty feet

of hungry water. There is only a line of someones,
heaping dirt on the breaking point. We try to fill
the belly of a flood with our little buckets.
Soon everything will be a swallowing.

Heretic

Offer me your prayers, those white
solvents. Offer me communion, little slips

of dynamite. Stroke my throat to help me
swallow. Tell me of winter, fields

sawed flat with cold, and I hear *ch–ch–ch*,
the antline of your marching, the way

any one of you is useless. Tell me
desire is a devil. Watch as I claw an orange,

sucking pulp free. My legs open to the sun
in its hard heat. I am dumb with wanting.

Desire like an iron nail, desire that could
split maple. I am strung. Watch me stretch,

toe to rib. Keep your hands. Keep your
promises. I'll bite off anything you place

on my tongue. Say I was a song you once
loved. Leave your bible on the table.

Let your key whisper in the lock. I trace
through pages, caress the red letters, luminous,

capital, vines galloping a prophet's body,
a bush in pure flame. I tear these out

to add to my bed, little strips gnawed
to a fine warmth. I curl up, wrists

rubbing one against the other, and sleep,
safe in my cricket-song, shivering.

Already

we are failing him. Someone has exams
& can't make the funeral. Someone brings

damp potato salad, which no one eats. Someone
brings lasagna but only three servings.

Someone's cologne stinks of cinnamon.
Someone's wife says *suicide* in a too-quiet room.

In his house, pink peonies that seemed so bright
now spill like clots from my arms, a choke

of baby's breath & green tissue that I heave
from the back step. That is where I find him—

alone, bourbon in its cradle of ice, best suit
draped under a plaid flannel. This is the moment

of apology. This is my chance to do this right.
My hand out, *Your mother,* I say, but he already

speaks, focused on thawing fields. Frostbit nights,
he tells me, she'd send him out with blankets

& *I'd worry, which for which. Save the blue wool
for my favorite.* She had told him not to be a fool.

All the beast feels is warm, or less warm.
My fingers pluck at the horse hair on his coat.

He shivers. *Do me a favor,* he says. *Make
a list. So I know who was here.*

Drink

As slaughter holds a lamb,
    as the lamb holds blood,
        as blood holds iron,
    as iron holds rust,
so this meaty corrosion
    is held in your mouth
        to be swallowed—
    but before swallowing
to be caressed, air drawn
    over your tongue, over
        this shallow of scotch
    in your jaw, as if the scent
walked on water, and yes,
    let's speak of it that way,
        God, Jesus, the Holy Spirit,
    yes, let's worship in terms
of proof, age, thirty years
    going on thirty-one,
        Aberlour versus Glen,
    Paul versus John,
let's assign the sharp,
    the honeyed, let's give
        the Baptists Oban—
    loam, moss, peat,
let's talk of the ground,
    let's lie on the ground,
        let's talk about resurrection
    and have another round,
let's talk for hours
    before you sober up,
        my darling, my disciple,
    before you remember

how you spoke of oak
        and sherry caskets, which
                produced a better flavor,
        and not one of your friends
asked if you meant *cask*.

This Silver Body

A man is gutting this fish on your walk to work.
      Or, your walk to work goes past a man who is
            sluicing his knife like sharp water to these gills.
      It's a sticky day. You put your briefcase down.

He is kneeling off the porch, over newspaper,
      but instead of changing a bicycle chain
            ropes of intestine reel out of this silver body
      and still you want to ask, *What speed?*

You hope for one last flop as he severs the spine.
      You hope for a steam burst as he slits this heart.
            There's just this click of ice as he packs the belly.
      There is no smell except your rancid coffee

in its cooling cup. He flicks loose yellow gel.
      You clear your throat because if it's shad,
            this might be roe. But he begins to hum,
      deep-fried baritone, and picks up the next one.

He slips a thumb in that eye for a better grip.
      He bounces that weight to his palm. He rolls
            both shoulders against the ache of morning.
      You're learning this was never for your sake.

The Door

After the work of T.D.

Enter the cathedral
& three spires crumble.

You take it as a chapel—
you lose the roof.

Accept this confessional:
Two walls are torn away.

Settle to a pew. The seat
collapses under you.

Kneel before the altar,
then the altar topples over.

Pray to the patron saint &
the statue's head is stolen.

Take him as a martyr &
someone lops off his arms.

In an empty field you eye
a lump of bodiced stone.

You came to worship
& now what do you hold

in your tight mouth?

What proves holy: space

or the architecture that inflects it?

Here is the church, here

is the steeple: a child
opens the door of her hands.

Inside, those people
never let her down.

August

Sooner or later, the thing you value most will beg to be burned.
Trust me, says the phoenix, *I'm immortal.* Watch your childhood
home—how the wires fray, how the baseboards splinter to tinder.
Your nights are split open by steam and the writhing of hoses.

Your sister learns to thicken gasoline with jelly, collects canisters;
the man you love shares a mouthful of smoke with someone else.
Trust me. Even Joan of Arc, age ten, tanned her arms as she tended
the sheep. *I'm immortal.* Tomorrow will rise to a full boil but still

you'll strip down, lay out, you'll slick the thin oil over your chest.
For six nights before the city blazed Nero could not sleep, pacing
the palace balcony. He fiddled to ease his nerves. *Pretty tune*,
whispered Rome: lips licked with flame, mouth readying to sing.

photo by Andrew Lightman

Sandra Beasley won the 2007 New Issues Poetry Prize for her book *Theories of Falling*, selected by Marie Howe. Her poems have also been featured on *Verse Daily*, in journals such as *32 Poems, Blackbird, New Orleans Review*, and *Meridian*, and in the 2005 *Best New Poets*, selected by George Garrett. Awards for her work include the 2006 Elinor Benedict Poetry Prize from *Passages North* and fellowships to Vermont Studio Center, Virginia Center for the Creative Arts, the Jenny McKean Moore Workshop, the Indiana University Writers' Conference, and the Millay Colony for the Arts. She lives in Washington, D.C., where she received her M.F.A. from American University and serves on the editorial staff of *The American Scholar*.

The New Issues Poetry Prize

Sandra Beasley, *Theories of Falling*
2007 Judge: Marie Howe

Jason Bredle, *Standing in Line for the Beast*
2006 Judge: Barbara Hamby

Katie Peterson, *This One Tree*
2005 Judge: William Olsen

Kevin Boyle, *A Home for Wayward Girls*
2004 Judge: Rodney Jones

Cynie Cory, *American Girl*
Barbara Maloutas, *In a Combination of Practices*
Louise Mathias, *Lark Apprentice*
Bradley Paul, *The Obvious*
Heidi Lynn (Peppermint) Staples, *Guess Can Gallop*
Ever Saskya, *The Porch is a Journey Different from the House*
Matthew Thorburn, *Subject to Change*
2003 Judge: Brenda Hillman

Paul Guest, *The Resurrection of the Body and the Ruin of the World*
2002 Judge: Campbell McGrath

Sarah Mangold, *Household Mechanics*
2001 Judge: C.D. Wright

Elizabeth Powell, *The Republic of Self*
2000 Judge: C.K. Williams

Joy Manesiotis, *They Sing to Her Bones*
1999 Judge: Marianne Boruch

Malena Mörling, *Ocean Avenue*
1998 Judge: Philip Levine

Marsha de la O, *Black Hope*
1997 Judge: Chase Twichell